A Girl,
Her Pen,
And These
Tear Stained
Pages

Rachel Freeman

A GIRL, HER PEN, AND THESE TEAR STAINED PAGES

Published by Rachel Freeman, Edmonton, Canada

ISBN:
Paperback   978-1-77354-732-9
ebook   978-1-77354-737-4

Publication assistance by

PAGEMASTER
PUBLISHING
PageMaster.ca

IS THERE A THEME,
PROBABLY
BUT I MAY BE BLIND TO IT
I MAY NOT BE ABLE TO SEE THE PATTERN
BECAUSE I AM FOCUSED ON SURVIVING THE
PAIN
NAVIGATING THE HURT AS IT COMES
AVOIDING THE INEVITABLE
HEALING THE INCONSOLABLE
IN WHATEVER FORM IT COMES
IN WHATEVER STAGE OF LIFE
IF YOU SEE A THEME
I HOPE IT HELPS

THE FEARFUL FRIEND

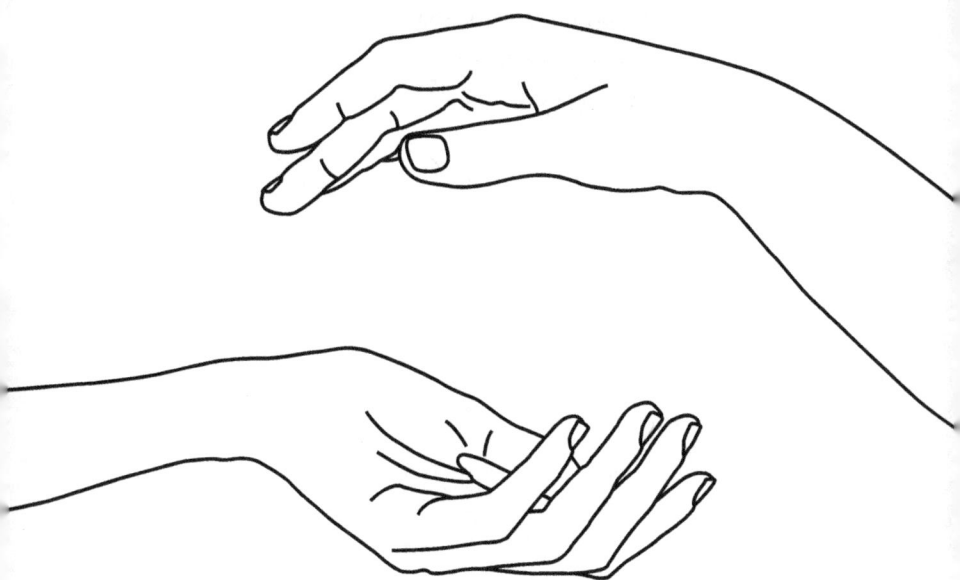

I think about you when I'm driving
Your memories disguised, hiding
Under the monotony of the task
The road running from my car tires
The engine working hard to keep me accountable
The radio droning in the background
Providing hit and miss soundtracks for the
pictures scrolling across my vision
Do you know I think about you when I'm driving
"We met through music... she was the drums
to my guitar, the beat to my heart"

A best friend is quite a naive concept
It's a young person's game
A whirlwind combination
Of belonging and betrayal

We would ignore the dependency
We would embrace the trauma
And it didn't wear us down
It didn't erode, or damage
It fueled our drunk adventures
It sparked our late night confessions
It brought us closer together
While shredding any potential for dignity

We didn't see what we didn't want to
And we didn't feel what we didn't touch
I see now and I feel now
This is why I didn't see the knife until you pulled it out
And as I stood there hemorrhaging
Desperately trying to hold back the landslide of despair
You simply, effortlessly whispered

"You took what was mine"

I never noticed the sharpness of your tongue
until it was my skin you were slicing

Safer to be on the side of the manipulator rather than against them
And I stood by your side
Loyally sheathing your weapon
Cleaning up your messes
Mopping the blood of your victims
All unknowingly, blindly, ignorantly

I never noticed the lethality of your words
Until I stepped out from beside you
Stepped into the line of fire and felt the razor cut through me
From each lick of the metal

"There is no friendship; I can't trust you"

I will never forget the kindness you lacked
Or the impatience that seeped out of your gaze
I will always remember the pain you caused
With the absence of empathy

A boundary you saw as irrelevant
A boundary I saw as necessary

"Why do you always have to be so difficult"

I didn't know how horrible your words were
until someone showed me my worth

I didn't know how crippling your tone was
until someone spoke kindly to me

I didn't know the weight of your cruelty
until someone told me to stand up

I didn't know the depth of the wounds until I started to heal them

I didn't see how intentional you were in diminishing
me until I started to see it all

"You pretended to be my safe space"

I've said yes so many times
I've laid down and let you walk
You were accustomed to my compliance

I can see why 'no'
Left you shocked

I can understand your reaction
I cannot understand the continuation of your distance

I am learning to be okay with your decision to choose leaving

"I am no longer keeping the peace, I am now protecting my peace"

You can't take credit for this
And yet you try
I've grown because of you
But not the way you think
I want for myself, the things you didn't do for me
I need the peace because of your chaos.
I desire warmth because you are cold
I'll manifest my worth because I feel like nothing in front of you

"Protecting my Peace"

THE WORST WIFE

Where would I have been without the fire,

The flames of addiction,

The heat of self-loathing.

Where would I have been without the burning desire to self destruct?

I washed your touch off my skin with tears, vodka and him....

At times I've believed that your love was my salvation.

Those were the times I've never been so wrong.

Wrong about myself and what I was worth.

You took and never gave.

I loved and never questioned.

You reached out and I walked away

I opened and you shut down.

And there we were naive to the daggers.

Accepting of the distance.

There is nothing louder than your silence
Nothing sharper than the dull grunts
Nothing more punishing than the reward of glances even if they are
…empty
Still your presence is paralyzing
I can move, I've worked so hard to move, I have moved
And I can move, so why am I still here
Why do I still come back here

"I want more"

I painted the walls in crimson

Getting the colour for my canvas

From the blood running in my veins

Every stroke taking from me

Every brush giving to the art

"You were horrible to me"

I hated you for painting over the colours in my world;
I hated your beige and browns
I loathed the monotony

And yet I picked up the brush and joined you.

We ignored the differences,
The distance, the discrepancies between us
And highlighted the similarities:
The sexual tension
The smiles
The trauma bonding.
What a beautiful bouquet of ignorance and naivety.

Your words chime like a blood curdling scream in the blackness of
my fast beating, rage-filled heart: 'I want more'...
And I was not 'more'

The silence between us is deafening,
The space, the distance is suffocating,
The effort it takes to be angry is exhausting,
But the anger is so comforting,
The anger fuels the silence and distance.

"Did it make you feel better",
"do you feel better now that I said it" ....
No, yes... like a knife slicing through me.
It felt like you gutted me,
every sensation I had the moment before you said it
drained from my body
like colour draining from the world around me.
No, it felt gross and consuming.
Yes, the words provided a moment of relief,
comforting my crazy, taming the questions in my head,
silencing the steady beating of your omission and denial.... no, yes.
The dichotomy is deafening, crippling, a weight.
At least the knife was sharp enough I didn't bleed out,
at least you said the words, "I cheated",
at least you didn't follow it up with minimizations
or justifications this time. The oddest sensation is
having the wind knocked out of you and being able
to breathe for the first time in months. I exhaled and
everything I was holding in, all the things I should
have said, all the tension and clenching released.

I didn't notice until you left the room.

I didn't know I wasn't exhaling, I didn't realize I was depriving myself of fresh oxygen, of a brain reset, of peace and contentment, until the door shut behind you and the exhale became euphoric.

I didn't notice because in the hold I was surviving the tension, hiding from the stress, finding sanctuary from the screams in your silence.

I think I picked you because I knew deep down you couldn't love
me, not the way I should have been loved.

I saw your weapons,your red flags, your thorns, and I still fell.

Tripped over my insecurities and landed in your arms.

I think I picked you because I knew you would shred
my trust and self-respect every time you
iced me out.

I knew your silent treatment would be as loud as my
mother's and your scowl rivalled the disappointment from my
father.

I think I picked you because the hurt was excitingly familiar, and the
heartbreak was far more comforting than a love I knew nothing
about.

"Slowly my gaze rose from the crimson crime scene in my hands to
the blood smeared brick wall I kept smashing myself into"

Wanting something is different than needing it

I need air to breathe

Blood for my heart to pump

Oxygen to feed my brain

Food to sustain my body

I need sleep to rest and recharge

And I thought I needed you to understand me, to listen to me, to

hear what I'm saying

I now know I don't need you to

I want you to

I desperately want you to understand me

To hear me

To see me

To love me

But I don't need you to

"I need you; I don't know what I would do without you"

I hesitated, looking at his hand, memorizing
every line, every wrinkle, every memory of
pain, heartbreak, anger, and joy. He held it
palm up, fingers stretched, confidently as
though he has and could again hold the
weight of the world, or equally as heavy,
the weight of a broken heart. I don't think
he knew what he was asking of me, "you coming?",
he looked at me with those enticing eyes, those
eyes that kidnapped my attention while my
heart squirmed and tried to flee from the bone
and flesh in which it was held. The words that
came out of his mouth were grammatically a
question but the tone and conviction created
a statement, a fact, a declaration that filled my
head and all the silence echoing between my ears.
I placed my hand in his and followed behind as he
effortlessly moved twigs, tree branches and spruce
bows out of the way, making his own path, and
his own destination. I was in the dark about where
we were going, I was void of information, void of
fear and void of pain. I prayed only to the universe
to keep safe my future plans and my innocence as
I threw caution to the wind and was led into the
unknown by the nameless man who often plagued
the recesses of my unconscious. To relinquish control,
to loosen my grip, to stray away from instructions and
directions took every fibre of my being; every ounce
of strength I had left was channeled into the allowance

of placing trust in someone I barely knew, someone
who might not even exist. We walked and without
words I learned about him, his childhood, traumas,
scars (both visible and hidden), the memories behind
the laugh lines and the light that held him at a safe
distance from the darkness; a picture was painted
in the comforting silence between us, every stroke,
every brush line giving me more than I had ever asked
for. I was so warmly distracted by the connection created
that I barely noticed that we had come to a clearing,
a green space surrounded by trees that I could
only guess had been untouched by the disease of
human interference. As the woods reached for
the safety of the clouds, the greenery and wildflowers
were sheltered, safe and breathtakingly vibrant.
The breath was taken from my body when I saw
yellow lady slippers in the middle of the clearing,
so perfectly placed, as if on purpose, just for me.
I made my way over, walking ever so cautiously as
to not disturb the beauty around me. Pink roses,
white tulips, purple daisies, pussy-willows, dogwood,
birds of paradise... as I tried to keep up with the
varieties and colours, my mind frantically tried to
make sense of the scenery surrounding me... I couldn't,
it didn't make sense. A reality set in, in an attempt to
bring back control and a pain shot through me that
brought me to my knees. I shut my eyes to try to
stop the crippling effects of the pain, something
changed. I opened my eyes and darkness replaced the
beauty, the flowers, the man, the safety, the vibrancy...

it was all gone. The dark stillness of my room grabbed
my body and shook me back into the paralysis of
loneliness. I was wrong, nothing changed, I was still alone,
and you were still gone

THE BROKEN DAUGHTER

Just because you installed the buttons
Does not mean you get to trigger them at will

"I'm just saying…"

The irony is glaringly obvious
As you stand there
Miles away
Angry that you must yell
Screaming at me
About the distance you created

If only you could stop
If only you could
Start
Walking
Towards me

It takes away
The words you use
The tone behind the letters
That fall out of your mouth
So effortlessly
It takes away from my confidence
From my heart and soul
From my happiness

And you don't know
You aren't aware
That it takes away from

I've changed you in my head
I've changed the colors to neutral tones
The songs are no longer, the music fades
I had to repaint the picture of you
Not out of spite or pettiness
I had to change the picture for my sanity
You are no longer the person I knew
Or maybe this is who you've always been but I didn't see it
Maybe I didn't see it because of the filters I had
Maybe I needed to blur the disdain and malice you used to cut
those around you
I think that hurts more
My heart breaks more thinking that I was the one that changed
I never imagined that my journey of healing and loving myself
Would lead to a slow drip realization
Of all the things you do
All the cuts your words leave
All the screaming your silence creates
All the heartbreak you don't know that your love gifts me

I used to think you dying would be my greatest heartbreak
That I would shatter into the pieces of myself that I molded to fit
your approval
That numbness I felt was the loss of your love
That I could not overcome and adapt to a world that you didn't
exist in

But now I'm watching you deteriorate into anger
Lashing out, leaving open wounds with the blade that you release
from your mouth when someone asks you questions or greets you
Throwing lit matches into the piles of gasoline that you've hidden
in conversations
Denying us the reality of the situation
Denying the flames that lick and flash over us

I used to think death would be the hell
I couldn't live in

You inhale and she can't breathe
You numb with drugs and her skin is on fire
You run away and she chases
Begging, pleading you to stay
To feel, to be who you were before you hated who you are

I've watched this dance, this cat and mouse game for years
I've witnessed her destruction through your addiction
I hate you and I love her
I love you and I hate her

I became apart of the shadows
The ones that followed you and the ones that tried to comfort her.

The day you overdosed I think she died too; I haven't seen her alive
in years.

"I lost my mother to addiction when my brother was 14"

It's cruel
You being here
But not being here

It's cruel
Your physicality paired with your emotional betrayal

Yet a cruelty I know too well
A cruelty I love

"Of course you love her, she's your mother"

I hate this place
I hate the flood of memories
The visceral reaction
The tension travelling through me
Touching every vein and artery

I hate the happiness I once felt here
And the piercing reminder of laughter and love

I hate being here
I hate that I miss here

"I grew up here"

It's damning
The evidence against you
It's piling up
Busting open the briefcase
of the lawyer prosecuting your case

It's suffocating
The testimony filling my mouth
It's strangling every inhale
Limiting every exhale
Squeezing the life out of every ounce
Of connection we had left

"I've gone no contact"

You were my worst heartbreak
And my hardest boundary
The ice that poured from your presence made it easier to go no contact
But the warmth of our memories tried to melt the frigidity that you
became

I don't know how to grieve you because I was never told it was
okay to
I don't know how to say goodbye to you because I was always told
that I can never turn my back
I don't know how to protect myself from the sharpness of your
knife or the sting
Salt on an open wound, everything you won't say

I've come to know that to grieve this loss I must grieve the loss of
myself when I was with you

"But they are your family…"

I don't think you understand
What it's like on the darker side
Of your perception of our relationship
I don't think you see
That we aren't okay
We aren't happy
This isn't functional anymore
I don't think you sense
The distant you've created
The loss I'm grieving quietly
The loudness of your delusions
I don't think you see me
Reaching for you
Desperate for attachment

"…So please don't take my sunshine away"

I don't love to hate you
I love to torture myself

"I got it from my mother...."

I wish she had kinder words
For herself and others
I wish her voice wasn't laced with the poison of resentment
From a lifetime of being told her flaws shine brighter than her
accomplishments

"I wish she loved herself the way I love her"

To my Mom

I'm sorry that they hurt you
With fewer words than none
I'm sorry that you're tired
Even though you're numb

I'm sorry they didn't hold you
When you didn't understand
I'm sorry that they punished you
And pushed away your hand

I'm sorry that you don't feel love
And didn't from the start
I'm sorry that I can't hear you
Through the silence in your heart

I'm sorry they gifted their pain
And made it your fault
I'm sorry they didn't believe you
And only added salt

I'm sorry I can't heal you
When the days are really bad
I'm sorry my hug isn't enough
And only makes you sad

I don't know how to say I'm sorry
For the pain I didn't cause

I'll be here when you're ready
I'll wait for you in the pause

"She taught me how to heal with all her broken pieces"

I didn't know what else to do so I started singing; the song she sang with me for years. I was years younger than I am now and at times I feel no wiser. She sat in front of me, watching me sing and clean, tidy the things she couldn't, organize the things she didn't see, dust the surfaces she hadn't touched, vacuum the floors she couldn't walk on, my grandma: the woman who helped raise me, the woman who helped raise us all. There she was and yet I couldn't see her, I tried but I didn't recognize her. "We did that," she said as the smile grew on her face, "we used to sing didn't we?" I don't think she was asking me; I think she was desperately asking herself, her own brain, in the hopes that she would remember, that something would click and it would come back.

"The dementia has progressed faster than we expected"

There are so many books I could read
To help me through the process
Of saying goodbye to you while you're still here.
There are so many words that others have written about the loss of
a loved one.
And yet I find little solace in these resources
I can't pull myself out of the pain of wanting your love long enough
to see that you're not actually here anymore
I can't understand how I'm supposed to bury you 6 feet under
when you're still 6 feet tall

"The challenge is to learn to live with the ambiguity"

This attachment has always come with conditions
There have been strings I thought were there to guide me
Instead they enslaved me
To be the mirror image of everything you wanted me to be
Your whipping girl
Your dumping ground
Your beaten dog

"Your broken daughter"

THE GIRL THEY TOOK FROM

I'll teach my daughter 'stranger danger'

It was never a stranger...

There's no way my daughter would let that happen to her

I've never let anyone do anything...

I'll show my daughter the difference between right and wrong

I knew it was wrong every time...

I'll make sure my daughter knows how to dress properly

I promise you, attire does not matter...

Oh my daughter knows to scream if anyone tries that

My voice was the first thing they buried...

She knows how to say 'no'

Their entitlement of me was far louder than my "no"

"I had nothing to give... that didn't matter"

The hypocrisy of my trauma and the insecurities it's created; the double-edged sword of being used for your body as a child and a teen and now as an adult believing they won't love me if they don't use me. The cut that leaves, the gash straight through the middle of my core, that feels irreparable most days.

They took whenever they wanted; whatever they wanted. And now... I beg you to take what I'm offering: I beg you to show me love. That's the way she learned.

"Men only want one thing"

The first time I was too young to fully comprehend, I was four

The second, a classmate for months while I watched the frog leap
on the computer screen

The third time they called it an "age-appropriate curiosity", "sexual
interference"

A teenage love, a first love; I can't remember the number of times I
said no

A man who called himself family

I've lost count
They all took, and what did they get
Pieces of me
Like candy smashed out of a piñata
Scrambling and taking

"Did they see that I had nothing to give"

A flash bang

The abrupt intrusion of the memory

The force of a thousand battering rams. If I was standing it

would have knocked me to my knees. I was stuck, frozen;

screaming but silent.

I had a piece of you that you never should have gave me

I didn't understand

"What I thought never happened, happened"

The letters don't understand their importance, the job they have to perform, to act out the script inside my mind. The words form the perfect expressions without insight or intention. The dance I have orchestrated for the sole purpose of turning my pain into pages…

Taking shards of myself back in the power of writing
Finding those parts of me they thought were theirs

"The pieces they took"

THE MOTHER

I dreamt of my babies before I had them.
I dreamt of my two boys and their adventures.
I dreamt of my first child and our bond.

But I never could have dreamt, I never could have imagined you.
You are the most incredible, empathetic, brilliant, adventurous,
joyful, caring, loving boy. You are the best pieces of all those
around you, you are everything I want to be and you are showing
me every day how to be a better mom and a better person.

I know I say stop growing up and you always say, "I can't!"
You're right buddy. Don't stop. Don't stop learning. Don't stop
growing. Don't stop loving. Don't slow down. Soak it all in.
Don't stop showing the world that living life in the fast lane doesn't
mean you're missing things; it means you're experiencing as much
as you can before you can't.

I can feel the pieces of myself shatter, crack, break apart with every inhale. These inhales aren't for more oxygen, they don't serve the purpose of feeding my brain to gain clarity or mindfulness. These inhales are cruel, sharp, consuming. Unrelenting in their goal to kill the hope in my lungs. These inhales catch the sobs hidden under them, trap them and hold them down, two hands on their neck, just the right amount of pressure and they only let go when the tears... stop... moving.

A kill that serves the sole purpose of making sure they don't see you cry. Don't let them see you break.

You're Mom

You get up and get them dressed.

You feed them and bathe them.

You have the answers and the right questions.

You are needed for story time and bedtime.

You will play with them and cry with them.

You can't break because they make you whole.

You can't fall apart because you're holding them together.

You're mom.

Kill the tears, ignore the murderous inhales, and get up.

I wonder how many times my mom cried under sunglasses
Coughed to cover the sob desperately climbing the back of her throat
The heartbreak and disappointment searching for release

I wonder how many times I sat in the back seat, behind her
A young girl tapping her foot to the beat of another 90s four chord song
Oblivious to the context of the waves of pain emulating from my mothers body
Clueless as to the words behind the heavy sighs coming from her silence

Let him be
Let him fly
Let him seek

What's it called
How's it work
Take a peek

Do not ask
Do not beg
Do not speak

Let it go
Let him question
Leave it be

He will climb
He will swing
Let him leap

You are worried
He is fine
That's the key

Always curious
Always wondering
Let him be

This is life
This is love
Never bleak

What is this
What is that
He will see

He will live
He will love
Let him be

Give me my baby

Can't they see me

Give me my baby

Can't they hear me

It's now a rhythmic drumming

Give me my baby

Breathe, deep breaths

Give me my baby

Am I screaming

Or whispering

Give me my baby

I can't stop the avalanche;

His cries and whines pick at me,

stab at my heart,

poke at my brain.

Why don't you understand?

Don't you remember?

I'm falling apart,

Give Me My Baby;

not the drums... my heart.

The rhythm is my heartbeat.

Give me my baby.

It's low at first

Then it quickens

Galloping

The screaming is ringing in my ears,
the screaming is my ears, wait.
The screaming is in my head.
The rage is locked behind my gritted teeth,
caged within the clenched jaw.
But it's so real I want to scream.
Yet there I sit, legs crossed,
sitting on my hands, smiling
and all that comes out of the prison cell
where the rage resides is a fake, forced chuckle.

I'm pleading…

Give me my baby….

Please give me my baby

Make it make sense
Make the answer match the question

"Does this mean you'll keep him from me"

Ask me something I can comprehend
Say it again but slowly

"Does this mean you'll keep him from me"

When did I ever

I wish someone would have prepared
me for the guilt. The plague that takes
over your body when there is a momentary
thought of "am I screwing this up? Am I
screwing them up?" The little people who
look to me for guidance, am I leading them
to heartbreak or failure? It's so quick too.
Less than a second, less than the time it
takes to blink. The feeling starts with
questioning curiosity and shifts into
crippling shame. Your own brain, the
organ inside your skull, the captain of
your ship, abandons you, walks out, turns
its back. Then you are alone, in a dark room
filled only with every disgusting, degrading,
vile intrusive thought you've ever had.
The dark is on purpose, not cliche, the dark
keeps you unaware of what thought is coming
next, bumping into you with the element
of surprise. There you are disoriented and
afraid and yet somehow comforted by the
familiarity of the thoughts,
like you've been here before

It all came easier
The love, the pain and the words
They all flowed so elegantly
Without effort or hesitation

And now?
Now I can't find two words that go together
I don't know how to put this pain into a sentence
I can't seem to type this out
Because it's not mine
It's his
You hurt him, you've left him

And as his mother, I feel powerless

He asks about you less everyday
Wonders where you are
Or what you're doing
He brings your name up once in awhile
Never with the same affinity as before but with a new curiosity
I think the question for him now is about the process of reconciling
Making sense of your lack of presence
While attempting to maintain the blurriness of his memories

My question is how
How can you justify your actions when they lead to his broken
heart

"Family will always be there for us"

The sting is worse when you have babies
The sting of abandonment
The pain of rejection
The hurt of dysfunction
The cuts left behind
It's worse when you have babies
I cry for them
I sob and weep
I don't sleep
I ruminate and rage for them
Your words mean nothing
Because your actions showed me everything
I want to lay down and die
I want to stay in bed until the pain stops
I want to break something
I want to make you hurt
But I am Mom
So I get up
I brush off the residue
I wipe away my tears
I push aside my pain
So that I can

They need me but they don't see me
They say my name without intention
I speak but am not heard
They are hungry and I feed them
They are thirsty and I bring water
They need clothes so they are dressed
They need love so I give and give and give
Mom, can you get my toys
Mom, can I have a snack
Mom, can you play with me
Honey, where's my keys
Honey, what's for supper
Honey, where are you going?

"My mom has called herself 'dark matter'; I know what she means now"

How would you like me to share that piece of me? How do you
propose I extract that part of my heart? Surgically?

Emotionally?

Physically?

Mentally?

How can you ask me to be okay with that dissection knowing what I
went through, knowing how much I broke, twisted, hurt to bring
that part to fruition. How can you ask, no demand, state with such
conviction, that I need to split that with you.

How dare you expect me to be happy about this; how dare you
leave no room for understanding or patience for a mother's love.

"I want 50/50 custody"

THE RECOVERING DREAMER

Breathe in stability
Breathe out chaos

"Don't forget to breathe"

I thought I had to write a story
That the lines had to flow, and the words had to complete the
sentences
I thought my thoughts, even the intrusive ones had to compliment
each other in an order that brought specific clarity and
understanding. I thought you wouldn't get it if I didn't make it obvious

I thought putting my pain in this form meant being invisible again

"All the things I was wrong about"

The look she gave me, the formation that her facial features made. Pity, no... maybe sadness or was it a trained response. A therapist treating a therapist. Except in that room, on that couch I became those who I help, those who want to heal.

I thought it would be harder than it was. I thought she would have to ask the complicated questions.

"What did your parents miss?"

Five words, five simple words that triggered a flood of emotions and memories I had worked hard to forget.

Everything they missed, everything I wanted to forget, playing like a movie in my head. A horribly paralyzing movie.

I understand the look on her face
I understand why she looked at me like that

There's something lonely about the first snowfall. It reminds me of being a kid, laying on my bed and my mom would bring in my freshly washed and dried duvet, my big white fluffy duvet. And with the flick of her wrists, so effortlessly she would parachute the duvet over me and my bed. And as the fluffy white fell over me, for a moment, before she pulled back the blanket to give me a kiss, for a moment I was alone.

The hush that settles in as the snow piles and demands to stay is lonely and comforting; heavy and light; bright and dark. There is the presence of everything and nothing and I feel both. The weightlessness turns into a heavy death, killing everything underneath of it; slowly though, not fast, it takes time for the life of snow to choke out that which lies beneath.

I watch the snow fall with curiosity and envy: does it demand or is it allowed. The thought that Mother Nature may also struggle with this existential dilemma - the push and pull of wanting to settle in, to belong, but waiting for the opening, for the allowance and acceptance. Most people watch the snow fall and appreciate the beauty of it or curse the fatalities that follow its arrival. I see the flakes navigate the air, floating down, back, and forth, side to side and I can't help but wonder if they come on their own accord or if they were invited. Do the flakes stage a hostile takeover or does the cool autumn ground and its decaying leaves welcome them with gratitude and excitement; do the leaves welcome the heavy, fluffy white blanket.

My question is not exclusively for the snow, but the northern lights dancing across the night sky as well. Do the cooler temperatures and the frigid winter air work symbiotically to welcome the brilliant crystal colours as they bring life to the dark. Or is it the opposite, do the northern lights move in intrusively and abruptly, casting light where darkness slept uninterrupted and content.

Am I welcomed here, or do I demand a space for my presence simply by being here. Did the lights and I make our own place in this world; did we force the waters apart and split matter to exist.

A snowflake lands on my nose and I'm startled back to the bleakness of my current position. As I re-enter the house, we share I can't help but bring the existential question with me; am I welcome here, do I belong and fit or am I forcing myself to be here regardless of how those around me feel about my presence. Well not those, just you. Do you want me here.

I want to be the colour of the dancing lights; I want to paint the darkness and shine; I want to be seen with awe and captivation. I wish you saw me.

The rabbit hole, this rabbit hole is always the easiest for me to slip in to and follow all the way down, through every tunnel, around every curve and plummeting down every nausea inducing drop.

The rabbit hole where I convince myself that you don't love me, and the kids would be better off without me. The rabbit hole where I embrace the aloneness that only comes under the white fluffy blanket.

Depression is a cruel, unrelenting bitch; I don't remember inviting or welcoming its presence.

You're strapped to a bed, a white bed.
That which holds you still is invisible,
That which paralyzes your bones and
Cripples your soul is all in your head.
The task is to find a way to deafen the voices,
Quiet the screaming coming from your body
And do this without painting the white bed red...

When the rain comes, I no longer seek shelter
I dance as it washes away the pain of yesterday and the hesitation
of tomorrow

I wonder about my life at times.

was it written in the stars,

was it a perfect combination of devastation and love,

is it a fate yet to be determined.

Was I meant for this or did I fall into the perfect state of chaos.

Was the heartbreak and pain supposed to happen to create the fire
in which the Phoenix conquered and birthed from, or did my life
end up so close to perfect in a similar way that the explosion of a
star created the beauty that surrounds us.

I watch the same shows over
From beginning to end
And then again

I remember and anticipate
I'd like to think that knowing what's
going to happen provides a peaceful
dichotomy to the unpredictable train
wreck I'm living in

Am I too much? Have I asked too much of you? The words, statements feel like facts, concrete evidence: I'm too much, I ask too much. I know the moment all too well, so I sit back, reign in the landslide of emotions and words that want to run together freely out of my mouth and into the air, I stop them with no hesitation. I don't even stutter. Okay. Yes, I'm fine. No, you're right it's not important right now. Tell me about your day.

And then I listen…

No,

I dissociate with a smile on my face.

"Oh no, yeah, I'm fine"

Let's not forget the pain we feel when we are healing
Let's remember the scars of climbing
The blood, sweat and tears we sacrificed to be whole
Let's honour this
Because this is how we got here

"Why does it hurt to heal"

I wanted this my whole life
I wanted it to be my forever place
I wanted it for all the wrong reasons

"Why do I do this to myself"

The suspension
Between your love
And your dismissal
That is the worst feeling

"That is the only feeling I know"

THE HEARTBROKEN HEALER

I'm sorry I don't know how to love myself the way you love me. I'm sorry I shy away from your hug, and I question your kisses. I open an umbrella when you shower me with gifts, I hide when you are showing me affection. Sometimes I don't know why you love me that much; I don't understand the willingness or openness of your kindness and compassion for me. I can't always translate it into something I can fathom.

"I love you just the way you are."

Nobody ever warns you
About the loneliness of growing
Not growing old or growing up
Growing outward
Taking the space, you know you deserve
Reaching your roots to new dimensions
Filling the cracks with self-love and value
Spreading yourself out and inhaling everything you know you've
worked for
Embracing the opposite of trying to be as small as possible

It's quiet and isolating,
Speaking up and inhaling into all the corners of yourself

It's heartbreaking
Breaking through the walls that have kept you small and palatable

"You've changed, we don't even recognize you anymore"

This used to be my safe place
This used to calm me

The warmth running down my spine
Reminiscing with me, serenading me

Now this is where the demons come
This is where the war begins

Every morning torturing me with truth
Every droplet carrying a demon

Riding the water down every inch
Every piece I don't like or recognize

Every demon laughing at my pain
Exaggerating my anger

Water used to lull me
And now it laughs

"The intrusion is everywhere"

The worst of them all
The most painful and peaceful
The strangest and most familiar
The thought that creates the most upheaval
And provides some sadistic reasoning

There
You
Are

I wondered when you were going to show up again
I wondered why it had been so long
I was starting to feel stable
I was starting to worry

"What if they are better off without me"

She is incredible

She is resilient and vulnerable. She is the fire and the water; the wind and the dirt that hugs the roots of all the trees within her. She battles and fights, walks, and runs, cries and laughs. She is more than a woman, she is everything I want to be, everything I have been and everything I strive for.

"I met her late in life but at the right time"

In all my attempts to do better, parent better, teach better, feel emotions better, hold them better, speak to them better, love them better, I think I've forgotten myself. Not the version I am now, not the 34-year-old, I haven't forgotten her. I've forgotten the 4-year-old; the ponytail that's drooped to the side from chasing butterflies and chasing her dreams; the mud pies and muddy hands born of creativity and curiosity; I've forgotten why she said good night to Neverland, Peter Pan and Tink; I've forgotten the sparkle she had staring at the stars. I left her somewhere between the innocence and the trauma. I lost her somewhere between the tenacity and the tension. She broke somewhere between the imaginary friends and the tangible monsters.

And I am not me, without her

"Can you see your inner child?"

There is beauty in the silence

There is

Anger

Love

Betrayal

Peace

And there is beauty

"Just hold me"

It feels hopeless holding back the landslide of emotions. Pounding, screaming, storming the gates that are my lips. Yet here I am with my hands shaking, desperately trying to form words that aren't laced with venom or malice. Here I am holding the landslide, barely keeping myself together, frantically searching for the right thing to say.

"Why are you so quiet, nothing to say!?"

I fear success because of the fall
I fear the attention and the celebration because of the scrutiny
Raising my hand to be seen, raising my voice to be heard
It means I would be seen, and I could be heard
Terrifying, the thought of being seen and tripping into
disappointment

"Waiting for the other shoe to drop"

If I gathered all the people who said horrible things about me, all the nasty, hateful, deprecating things about me

If I gathered them into one room, one space with four walls, a floor and a ceiling

The voice in my head would still be the loudest, she would put them all to shame

"Why can't I be better"

The numbers have me in a chokehold; I'm paralyzed standing there, hoping something will change. Three numbers, lined up beside each other, just doing their job and yet I hate them. I loathe them and fear them. I've used them to punish myself more often than reward myself. I've sat with the feeling in my body, the numbers defining my outline, every curve and crevice.

The numbers haunt me.

"You have the face, just not the body"

I can feel myself unraveling

A slow disentangling of the pieces

The things holding me together

Methodically letting go of each other

I wish I knew how to stop it

And I want to speed it up

I want to be able to pull it all back together, stretching myself to

the limit so that I can reign it all back in

Or I want to disintegrate faster

Fall apart entirely

And in the rubble find solace

Peace in the nothing

No expectations

No voices

No demands

No needs

No wants

Nothing

Just the unravel

"Get your shit together"

4 minutes and 27 seconds, the amount of time it took me to spiral with no resistance into the depths of suspicion and distrust. Unwavering confidence in my paranoia; an unsettling determination avoiding all accountability and rationality. 4 minutes and 27 seconds and I convinced myself I would be alone again, surrounded by everything I hate. In 4 minutes and 27 seconds I packed your shit and begged you to stay; I screamed at you while whispering and pleading...

"Sorry babe, I was on the other line"

Sit with me and listen
Not to respond or react
But to observe the words I form
Hold space for my struggles and strains
Grieve with me, my loss of identify
Sit with me and hear my tears
Give them a place to stay and go
Gift my anger with acceptance
And my pain, show it belonging
Sit with me and see me

"I thought I was born to be a therapist; the reality was I became
what I needed"

She covered me with the white blanket

A symbol of her unity

And as it fell, I caught a glimpse of her smile, small yet powerful

From the corner of her mouth and the crest of one cheek

The intention was everything

Comforting, caring, loving

She didn't need me to be happy

She didn't need me to be grateful

She wanted me to know what I wasn't…

"You are not alone…You are the colour in our dancing lights"

Most days I am searching, wandering down different paths wanting different answers to the barrage of questions that infiltrate my brain. Uninvited guests that barge in, no couth or patience, needing to be heard in this moment, seen right now, "I'd like to speak to the manager" attitude. The questions needing answers before the thought is fully formed, the next question flying forward demanding attention. Most days I'm trying to find a reason why my brain works this way, why I can't live in boxes, why my elastic bands all touch and suffocate each other. Most days I wish I was different.

"What is wrong with you? Why can't you be normal?"

You know that feeling
That lonely complete feeling
That tingling sharp feeling
It's there when I'm in front of you
And disappears when you're gone

"Sometimes love hurts"

The thought of us ending
Of this ending
That thought is paralyzing

I've worked hard for this love
I've put in time with this love
I've changed in this love
I've grown in this love

After the years of heartbreak and self sabotage
Picking the beds of men who couldn't
Remember my name
Laying in the sheets of unkept promises and overused broken ice
After years of hating the picture that other people painted of me
After thousands of journal entries and empty vodka bottles

I've worked hard for this peace
I've put in time with this peace
I've changed in this peace
I've grown in this peace

This new love was a slow burn
A calculated inhale
A conscious invitation into my lungs
A long breathe
A beautiful ignition of light and wonder

Thank you for helping me believe in everything I was told wasn't
real
"This lifetime and the next <3"

All the versions of her stood in front of me; the 4 year old, the 8 year old, the 12 year old, the 15 year old and the 20 year old. Statues before me of my former selves; stone faces expressionless, cold and unexpecting. I blinked and they blinked back, the stone cracked and I began.

With confusion that grew into remission, they handed me their narratives with ease: watching me heal, hearing me tell their stories, detailing their pain and heartbreak, putting sound finally to the silence they've sat with, the feelings they've drowned in. They observed me with empathy and I spoke for them with tears racing down my cheeks.

They've been stagnant in their hurt, unheard, unseen, invalidated and dismissed, not only by the world, but by me…. And now there is warmth for them, reception for them, acceptance and authenticity in the words forming, flowing through me for them. Slowly, without warning, one by one, starting with the oldest they walked into me, molding into my body effortlessly. The 20 year old, the 15 year old, the 12 year old, the 8 year old… the 4 year old stopped short of the reconciliation, looked up at me with a smile that I could only compare to a sunflower on the hottest day in July, she said,

"I told them you'd come back, I told them you wouldn't forget"

I've walked with her in fields, vast spaces filled with wonderful colours and textures, walking to the pulse of the earths heartbeat, breathing in the songs of the birds surrounding us. We've run together, galloping with the wild horses, stretching forward, reaching for the peace that comes with being faster than your demons. We've climbed trees whose branches touched all the corners of the sky, framing the sun, holding its face in their hands as gently as they can. The roots pushing the dirt aside, telling the story of the tree's foundation, the stability of its beginnings, the sturdiness of where it all began. I've sat with her within the safety of our mind, sharing our thoughts and feelings, sharing our love of nature, surrounding ourselves with all that we wished for, that which we hoped for. I'll stay with her because she needs me; I'll stay here with her for as long as I need to.

"I love you; I will never leave you; I'm not going anywhere."

I have hidden her, ignored her, and left her alone. We were meant to be one, but the separation was involuntary; two bodies, two hearts, two sets of eyes. She's watched, and observed, intent on solving and predicting, while I protected and pushed through. The broken shards of her sense of self surrounding her, hovering, patiently waiting to do the damage they were intended for. I've watched, anticipating the forced entry, the piercing of her skin, the bloodletting that comes with self-destruction. At times I've participated in holding the daggers back, feeling them slice through my hands, push through me with intent: to get to her. Other times I've stepped aside maliciously, resentful of the pain she carries for us, seeing her struggle to hold back the sharpness of self-doubt, insecurities, and the inner hatred that comes with being used and abused.

I am the hurt, I am the pain she carries, I am the broken shards.

"A girl, her pen, and these tear-stained pages"

Thank you for completing
A Girl, Her Pen, And These Tear Stained Pages.

We would love if you could help by posting a review at your book retailer
and on the PageMaster Publishing site. It only takes a minute and it
would really help others by giving them an idea of your experience.

Thanks

PM Store Author's QR Code
https://pagemasterpublishing.ca/by/rachel-freeman/

To order more copies of this book, find books by
other Canadian authors, or make inquiries about
publishing your own book, contact PageMaster at:

PageMaster Publication Services Inc.
11340-120 Street, Edmonton, AB T5G 0W5
books@pagemaster.ca
780-425-9303

catalogue and e-commerce store
PageMasterPublishing.ca/Shop